three some poems

jeannine dobbs
kinereth gensler
elizabeth knies

Hearthstones
Copyright © 1976 by Jeannine Dobbs

Someone Is Human
Copyright © 1976 by Kinereth Gensler

The New Year and Other Poems
Copyright © 1976 by Elizabeth Knies

Library of Congress Catalogue Card Number 75-23819
ISBN: 0-914086-11-1
Printed in the United States of America

Cover designed by Marianne Quinn

Special thanks to New Hampshire Composition, Inc.

Alice James Books are published by
the Alice James Poetry Cooperative, Inc.

ALICE JAMES BOOKS
138 Mount Auburn Street
Cambridge, Massachusetts 02138

CONTENTS

HEARTHSTONES
by Jeannine Dobbs

CONTENTS

SOMEONE IS HUMAN
  by Kinereth Gensler

CONTENTS

THE NEW YEAR & Other Poems
  by Elizabeth Knies

Thanks are due to the editors of the following publications, in which some of these poems appear:

Jeannine Dobbs
Bridge; I, That Am Ever Stranger: Poems of Woman's Experience; The Little Magazine; The Ohio Review; Pearl; Penumbra; The Wormwood Review

Kinereth Gensler
The Blacksmith Anthology, Fire-Exit, Grist, New Orlando Poetry Anthology, Poetry Northwest, Prairie Schooner, Sequoia, Stonecloud, The Virginia Quarterly Review, Women/Poems, Yankee

"English Is a Foreign Language" appeared in *Best Poems of 1973* (Borestone Mountain), Pacific Books, Palo Alto, 1974

Elizabeth Knies
The Hudson Review, Lancaster Independent Press

Grateful acknowledgment is made for use of three lines from "The Landlord" by Boris Pasternak, as translated by Robert Lowell in *Imitations,* copyright 1961 by Robert Lowell. Reprinted by permission of Farrar, Straus & Giroux, Inc.

HEARTHSTONES

Jeannine Dobbs

Jeannine Dobbs

THOSE SUMMER EVENINGS

Downstairs the shuffling of grownup voices
Their cards falling like soft rain

Overhead the play of leafshapes —
the streetlamp shining through our maple

At my window a white blur
batting the screen
like a pebble thrown
over and over

Pushing the sheet down
pulling my gown up
reaching into the cool half of double bed
where no one yet had slept but mother.

THE COMPANY MAN

Yoo-hoo, he'd call
striding in unknocked
Mother and I banging
together behind him
like baggage

He liked to visit
the real butter and cream
the extra layer of devil's food
He'd tell the story
he was good at

After dinner he'd excuse me
meaning, Get lost
within calling distance
Don't break anything
important, a lamp
a leg
that would have to be
noticed.

Jeannine Dobbs

THE INHERITANCE

Lavender is what I remember
or try to
Lavender hair
lavender-water
and gold
a touch of 14K
at her ears
She handled me with kid gloves
on if she had to
None of those floury hands
rocking chair laps
and fairy stories
I never saw her get old
she was old
She made piano lessons
sound like a debut at Carnegie
Later Mother told me:
her man and the money
gone with a henna-haired woman
We gave her
Sunday

Grandma lies on a bed
that smells like a baby's
I've never seen her without earrings
She doesn't know me either
When widow Gratz's boy
rolls on the floor and slobbers
Daddy sits on his chest
sticks a spoon in his mouth
and sends me to the car

Driving home the half moon
is the color of skim milk
Daddy sings
Casey Would Waltz/
With the Strawberry Blonde/
While the Band Played On

If I felt like singing, he'd say
You got that tin ear
from your Mother.

Jeannine Dobbs

HAIRBRUSH POEM

I am sitting once more
in the hard chair
of childhood
and Mother is trying to unriddle
my hair
 It keeps snarling
 and clenching its fists
Mother, what did you see in me?
Was it the face you wanted to see in your mirror?
The face you wanted to fit in your locket?
You should have had your own dreams
but you'd already given up
sleeping by then
 To this day I still prefer
 rats' nests
 to that bed of pins
 you urged me
 to lie down in.

DISCOVERY

Here.   See?   Here in the clearing —
mushrooms! Edible
sponge,
big floppy ones
like sunhats
    They take me back
to following my Mother's faded gingham
bordered with new rickrack
Me, an acolyte
in middy blouse, Indian belt, cuffed
jeans, scuffed saddles...
These, she would say
finding a cache, a colony,
a fairy ring
Our ears would fairly sing with bees, mosquitoes
Over here!   I hear her,
see her kneel to fill our woven willow baskets
She and I alone
together inside barbed wire strands
surrounding the last vestiges of virgin land
She showing me how to tell a morel
(dark with a honeycombed cap)
from a toadstool
Wise from the Depression
Mother, thinking mushrooms
something I should know

Jeannine Dobbs

I thought I could learn nothing new
from her. But then
it was fun
That was thirty years ago
in another state,
but still I know the difference.

See.   These, these are safe.

KITCHEN SONG

Trust a woman
to conjure joy out of pain,
out of that room I thought I'd never
want to see again. That citadel
my Mother banned me from —
sacred as her bedroom
(that private estate
of drawn shades
and headache).

My Mother's kitchen.   Where my hands
betrayed me: too big,   too slow,
dirtying too many pots,
forgetting if I'd put in a pinch
or not. Her parings
were all of a piece, whole-cloth,
a magician's trick
I couldn't be taught.   My knife
seemed eternally aimed
straight for wrist or heart.
You'll be no man's wife.   Get out.

My kitchen.   Pots of dirt
for herbs: rosemary, thyme
and flowers.   Hand-potted dishes
lined up for the kittens
(yes, Mama, they have their own);
the coffee's on
and there's a man who'll eat
my success or my failure. Come,
Mama, into my kitchen —
Here's a slice
of sun and a song.

18

Jeannine Dobbs

FIRST MEETING

Now I knew why the trip had been so slow —
it was the kind of place no one hurried to get to.
Even the road had given up before it got there,
yet the house leaned as if once the wind
had tried to get in.   Looked at through tears,
the green tarpaper disappeared
into grass and trees, but the porch was real
and the washing machine.   The screen door
had no screen, but inside
gray linoleum and daisied plastic curtains
gleamed. The father was wearing my husband's
nose. "Where's the baby?" the mother asked.
But we hadn't made any.

SNACK

We have slept together
over fifteen years and yet
there is something intimate
in finding ourselves
here in the midnight kitchen

You make a tent of my hair,
act the boy, your mouth
has already taken on the morning
taste of a penny
We sit at the table to discuss
the merits of milk over beer,
jape at the pickles
naked in jars

       Tomorrow
this crust I leave on my plate
will still seem to be smiling.

Jeannine Dobbs

COFFEE, BLACK

You slam your cup
in its saucer —
the fist
you never pound
in your palm
my face —
My Father's gesture
swallowing his rage
for fifty years
nourishing the raw wound
he grew in his stomach

I am fat with guilt
Spit out
the black, hot, strong
words you spoon down

Let there be knives
to keep your hands busy
at the surface
away from your mouth.

NEIGHBOR

Every street has at least one
woman the children run from
You can see her daily in her yard
watching trees grow,
feeling with her eyes how the slow moss
nestles at roots,
listening to cars go by
telling their secrets to the road
Only a one-footed chickadee comes to her hand
who wears her one smile and same drab
coat and woolen snood and gazes
through her opaque eyes at wood
She does herself no harm
and would wish all who pass
if she remembered
that they lie down hungry
and rise up full.

Jeannine Dobbs

FOR RUSTY

You are against everything
soft, now,
even chairs
I usually find you
dumped on the floor —
a discarded doll —
the way he
left you
with 2 kids
in the same bed —
that was 2 years ago —
he still pays just enough
to keep you
from relief
Somewhere you muster extra
to maintain your one
vice — your hair, that torch
that shows you still care
You may give the finger
to the world, Raggedy Ann,
but under that denim shirt
your very real heart
still hurts.

OZARK FARM WIFE

O sweet Jesus she sings
to the one-eyed dog from a forgotten fair.
She smooths the quilt of the deep-troughed bed
wishing him home from harvest.
Each year following fall to the west
for winter money.   Each year coming back
slower.   Meantime she lowers
to the well and hauls to the porch
where the white machine squats
mortgaged on the rotted floor. O sweet
Jesus in the feathered air
and nothing left but chickens to do.

Jeannine Dobbs

PORCH

Rainy days
this deck
ploughs through restless
spirea,
gently lists to starboard

Yearly refuge
for finished Christmas trees,
the same phoebe —
I know it's the same phoebe —
The rusty song
of the swing,
the ivy whispering
to lovers

Pure schlock

Don't knock it!

PARLOR

What am I waiting for?
Something special enough
to happen?
Nothing is ever special
enough

> I can't get past the lintel...
> The twilight room is gone
> that was once as real
> as these lilacs
> outside my window
> with their scent
> of nineteenth-century gentlewomen

I've resolved, again, to live
only in the present moment;
that the next time love comes —
that funnel,
that twister —
to open myself
like a window.

DINING ROOM

Gather your knees under the meat
It is the hour of together

The strong find their own places
The weak are directed by Mother

Father gets the first cut
Pass the sweetest to Mother
to neutralize her tongue
Pass the water to the smaller,
tell them it is broth to make better
Be sure they are grateful
forever and ever

It is polite to keep one hand
in your lap
to catch the droppings
Do not diddle
at the table
When you have finished,
fold your knife and fork
over your empty plate
to keep the devil
from his dinner.

KITCHEN

O
lemonscented
honeybreathed
crisp
children
licking chocolate
fingers, proud
copperbottomed
sun and freshly starched
breeze spilling
into the apple
and vanilla
checked gingham
room, the good news
man on the radio...
No
   ...the potato
prances in the pot
like a missionary,
wanting out.

CELLAR

Dusky bin
The lid is on
This is the place between waking and sleeping
where the leg jerks with a will of its own

Why is it the children among us
are holding their breath?
Is it that the same air
is used over and over?

The house settles overhead
like a woman folding her gloves in her lap
before speaking
or a bat folding its wings before sleeping

Here there are no arms
but your own arms
Nor ever.

BEDROOM

A hall of doors
This one?
That one?
Choose one
How do I know what is behind?
How do I know which to choose?
Choose

Beyond the door
a room with a couch
and a man —
What does he have
in his hand?
Is it a Tootsie Roll?
Is he the Sand Man?
The Dream Man?
Husband? Analyst?
Father? Lover?
Go ahead   Choose

*Didn't your Mother
tell you?*

BATHROOM

Dependable
Efficient
Relatively quiet
How many times
has a toilet failed you?
A toilet is a toilet
whether you are using it or not

Just so,
I am trying to learn
how to remember
I am a woman
whether anyone is
loving me or not.

CLOSET

A true democracy

Or, a woman's kind of place:
the rack and hanger
satisfy her need for
order

Wallflowers
Waiting to be chosen

It is possible to be lost
whole seasons
and not even know it.

Jeannine Dobbs

ATTIC

This ark
rides the floodtide of wind
Branches beat against the roof
as if the carpenters' hammers
were still tapping

The dove has not returned to this steeple

Here there is one of everything
and may be needed.

SOMEONE IS HUMAN

Kinereth Gensler

for Walter

Kinereth Gensler

ENGLISH IS A FOREIGN LANGUAGE

English is a foreign language I was born speaking,
a place I live in, like my house

and, like it, foreign to my waking feet
that slide to the edge of morning without knowing

what floor they'll touch — which house,
what hemisphere. Or if the floor will tilt

and they again will find themselves on deck,
waiting for winches to lower the lifeboat.

The one sure speech I know is born of water.
It comes in answer to foghorns, sirens, bells —

vibrations that a foot responds to.
It is the sound of total breath released

when, poised above stopped engines, one first feels
the pumps take hold.

I wake each morning as I woke then,
speaking the language of the new undrowned.

FOR NELLY SACHS

Every morning I took a shower
Every morning under the hot spray
tuned by my hand
I saw the valves
streaming gas
from the walls and ceilings
of rooms marked "BATH"
in Buchenwald   Bergen-Belsen

As if I'd been there
As if it were required of me
As if all Jews
were forced to start each day
stripped in a locked room
remembering in their skins
unable to stop it
just as one by one women
like me had stood
packed in a locked room
under the streaming gas
unable to stop it

    Give us this day
    the grace
    of showers

I can't remember when it stopped
In the crush of body-counts
in the years of drought & floods
& saturation bombing
I lost them all
they went up
in numbers

Kinereth Gensler

O the showers Nelly
the showers
where I stand alone   graceless

This numbness
like the end of all desire
the terrible forgetting in my body

JERUSALEM OF STONE

I

You could be blind here.
Among the rough stone walls
and the smooth dressed faces of houses
you could be Isaac,
taking your cue from stone.
The voices of Jacob and Esau

call from opposing rooftops.
You stand at the Western Wall,
separate, a woman
torn between rams' horns
and the minaret's loud speakers.
You touch the stones. You listen.

In this city of many layers
where each new war
uncovers earlier stonework
and the steps go down to bedrock,
the sun still walks on the walls
and the tower of David.

Late in the afternoon,
when he walks on his rooftop,
you could, without loss, be a stone,
unquestioning in the light,
washed in its radiance only,
blind as Bathsheba bathing.

II

what I know of stone:

how it is sun
after the sun goes down

how cold overcomes it
and it contracts
holding the crease of light
for eons if need be

how far quakes reach it
tremors
running beneath the sea & mountains
the pressure of trapped suns
building inside it and the shrug
the long & patient stone-shrug

how it shakes free and waits
crack by hairline crack
till blown seeds find it
anemone   cyclamen   me
held fast by this stone
flowering   holding it

III

rain is falling on
the Street of the Chain

it falls on the stone steps
on the open faces
of stalls and alcoves

41

it falls through the holes
it links one side
with the other

in the Armenian Quarter
the Barakat Brothers
the Moslem shopkeepers
the Jews are drenched
with the rain that is falling

the barbed-wire fence of
no-man's-land is gone
and the steps are slippery

the rain has no color

we are all up
to our necks in it

Kinereth Gensler

JOSEPH, FROM THE PIT

I will not tell my dreams.
I will not wear a cloak
different in any way from cloaks worn by my brothers.
I will not boast.
I will not show myself beloved.

Save me, my Lord.
And when you save me —
when the hands reach down into the pit and place me
in the sack for Egypt —
I swear that I shall be
as smoothed and brown and indistinguishable as seed-corn.

I will contain myself —
be useful, modest, grave,
telling only the dreams of others.
Not waste my seed
but pass from hand to hand as hard, strong currency:
coin of the realm,
the grain in which the market finds its base.

I will take an Egyptian wife, an Egyptian name,
and store up provender for Pharaoh.

And I will wait
until, in middle age,
my father sends for me.
Till Jacob in his mortal need of grain
sends those who sold me,
his ten sons — grown strange and bearded —
to barter with the smooth brown unknown face of Egypt.

Will I remember then this dream-devouring place?
Coated in Pharaoh's strength
will I know how to greet my brothers?

43

Save me, my Lord.
Surely I will not plague them long with childish games
but I shall split my face
and raise the full sheaf of my hoarded dreams
and go
and bow myself upon the neck of Jacob.

Kinereth Gensler

IN HIS LIFE, IN HIS DAYS

In my father's house
the mirrors reflect
my face

Everything's mirrors

Rare sunlight catches
my face in his cello
on the surface of paintings

I'm tucked in his blotter
in the bowl of his pipe

I pull myself out
book by book
from the shelves

It makes no difference

I'm filed with the letters
my face is the moon
in his silver Kiddush cup

To mourn
is to cover the mirrors
not see my face

To prepare for mourning

is to see his face
once, while there's time
only his face

THE BATH

My mother's eyes are tranquil.
She shreds bits of paper.
I give her more paper, more —
napkins, tissues, a forest.
She says Yes, I'm grateful,
I'm so fortunate in my daughters.

I run the tub.
I bathe her.
I scrub the shadowed place beneath her breasts.
She says Thank you my darling
you're so kind I love you.

In the moist, closed room
I see she is my grandmother,
the grandmother I never had:
a brand-new lady, dripping with gifts,
arrived in time for me to play with
like a baby

or a mother —
that unknown grandmother
who ripped the lining from her coat before she died
and gave this child who nursed her through the nights
all she had left to give:
a saved-up envelope of money.

I kneel on the mat.
The room dissolves me.
I become a pool of children, mothers, babies.
We pluck at coats.
We dip our hands in secret pockets.

The commandment floats, buoyant in water.
My daughter watches with her radar eyes.

Kinereth Gensler

FOG POEM

This or that, says the mind:
mountains, or the ocean;

a climate for lemons
or a climate for apples.

I

You come to the Bay
(chance takes you
or you're born there
like any stranger),
you come to a steep house near the ocean.
In front, there's a lemon tree;
in back, an apple.
Your windows face the great suspension bridges.
The weather is fog.

Fog is the sign of the Bay,
its first condition,
suspending the view for hours,
suspending vision,
condensing in fine, cool particles of water
on fruit trees and the bells of fuchsias,
bathing the small leaves of live oaks, entering
the fire-resistant core of redwoods.

You wait for the fog to lift
each day, unfailing:
the warmth on your skin, the sun
filling the air with bridges.

II

The Bay is elsewhere.
A hole in the mind remains,
an absence

where a tooth was.
Fog drifts
over the same old narrows,

under the isolated tips of towers.
It goes round and round.
It bangs its head against abutments.

You feel for the hole.
You reach behind it.
In the lurch of time and space

a real fog answers.
It lifts as it comes, it clears.
You touch the roadway.

Kinereth Gensler

A PRIVATE HOARD

I would enumerate and keep
from this year's wandering
a private hoard of birds,
used here as common coin but strange to me
as the vernacular is strange
to travellers abroad.
The canyon's marketplace of birds —
small change
as comes unasked for with a loaf of bread.

I would keep polished in my hand
the plain brown towhees
and the brighter ones with rufous sides;
black-hooded juncoes
and the chickadees with chestnut backs;
and kinglets, olive-green,
found twitching in the weeds;

Mourning doves, gray as the canyon's fog,
with empty jewel-holes on their wings;
mountain sparrows, variously streaked,
the pale rose breasts of finches
and the strong curved stance and beaks
of the uncrested jays,
the scrub jays of the West.

What can be packed and kept
that does not lose its sheen
or tarnish in the chest? —
A list. Some feathers.
The brush of words.

THE FABULOUS, THE EXTINCT AND THE REAL

Under the snow — in China, perhaps,
or Egypt, or the Mesozoic —
the birds gone from our skies
are wintering. Is it the Everglades
they nest in? Does Scheherazade
see them from her window?
I speak of them all: rocs,
pterodactyls and passenger pigeons
as well as storks and robins.
In this season, each
is as much gone as the others.

Somewhere it is spring: the times
and families of earth hold reunion. There,
where the globe splits along its seam,
a profusion of the possible occurs —
a continuum of wings.
I expect a messenger at any moment.
Tugging at worms, he will uncover
the crack in my garden.

DANDELIONS

Old woman
muttering up the road,
in queer shoes striding
along the highway with no sidewalks —
in a man's old felt hat
bending to pick unkempt grasses,
filling your market basket
at the edges where the power-mower
and the scythers cannot reach,
where the golf-course and the graveyard fences stop,
where unstunted dandelions, growing fiercely,
are greens for your dinner
and fat blond heads for your winter wine —

Driving that road
I see you move into my line of vision,
walking the highway's fringe,
defiant, picking.
I slow to pass —
you flicker at the rolled-down window:
the felt hat slips,
the gray fuzz on your head blows towards me, reaching.
I shiver in the bright June morning.

Our faces meet inside my rear-view mirror,
sister, June's indestructible blown weed.

SESTINA: AN OLD STORY

The child had 20-20 vision.
The clue was always there: that episode
where she picks wildflowers in the wood,
when, basket on her arm, she meets the wolf
and still won't hurry, still can't keep her eyes
from thickets where blue hyacinths lie hidden.

We see her next at the door, half-hidden
by flowers, basket, hood — a vision
from our first picturebooks. She is all eyes,
all innocence, a pawn in episodes
whose end is preordained: the wolf
is slain; she learns to fear the wood.

"Come in, my dear!" he cries, as we knew he would.
He's tucked in bed, his whiskers hidden
by Grandmother's nightcap, but he looks like a wolf.
Could any child, with even partial vision,
be fooled by such a flimsy episode?
Some secret lay behind that snout, those eyes,

some great unfolding. With her own eyes
she'd seen those wondrous changes in the wood,
watching a stone move (cautious, its head hidden),
watching the leaf with wings, the snake's episode
of shed skin. Do people undergo revision?
Old people? Grandmother? Is she this wolf?

Now (in that queer, high-pitched voice), the wolf:
"Come closer, child!" — "But, Grandmother, what big eyes
you've got!" (What ears! What teeth!) — Could she envision
herself transformed, made meek, incurious, or would
she wait to learn the secret hidden
from children until the final episode?

Kinereth Gensler

The hunter dominates that episode.
He does not hear her cries, he hears the wolf's
loud snoring. And she, swallowed alive, hidden
in that dark gut, sees through corrected eyes
how wrong it is to dawdle in the wood,
how dangerous to trust her small girl's vision.

She learns: Meet each new episode with downcast eyes.
Avoid: wolf, flowers, turtle, butterfly, snake, wood.
Be good. Be safe. Stay hidden. Abandon vision.

LIKE PORCUPINES

I have no love poems.

When I loved —
a long, long time
ago and still not past —
I had no need

for poems.
I make a poem
not in the way that I
made love, but care-

fully, and in some pain.

Kinereth Gensler

MOTHERS

In my day, they threw childbirth at us
saying, You owe me!

(an arm, a leg, your next paycheck
& all your love)

Relax, you owe me nothing.

It is enough to take the world,
incalculable, as it comes.

      Into my lungs,
      each morning.

PROLOGUE

If she could be their storyteller
she would.

Or if from mustard seeds
and wool-gathering she
could weave them bright blankets.

To be that Roman whose stone bridge
two thousand years
still spans the Tagus!
Or be that bridge.

She is instead a hostelry.
Knapsacks appear at her fire,
moments of singing.
Her rug is worn through near the firescreen
and her rooms breathe road dust.

They come and go.

O someday she will have
the youngest and most constant of
her heart's desires.

To be an old
and marvelous woman.

Kinereth Gensler

WHERE METAPHOR BEGINS

What is it that a heap of corpses looks like?
a heap of corpses looks
like a heap of corpses, like bodies, dead:
this woman, that, that child,
a heap of them, some flies, a sprawl,
a sprawled heap, a heaped sprawl: corpses.
You can do better than that. Try.
Matchsticks? — Flies don't settle on matchsticks.
Dolls? — Ditto for dolls.
Sleepers? — All at one time having nightmares?
Garbage?
It looks like itself, it looks
like nothing else on earth,
must not be let
to look like anything else on earth.
It is an element, most irreducible:
salt. A prime number.

PLAGUE

The locusts are swarming inside our children

They have waited us out, dormant
in their inexorable cycle
while we gave TLC & vaccines
against diphtheria, whooping cough, scarlet fever
against smallpox & poliomyelitis

They waited, patient as intelligence agents
till the children's teeth
were straightened and their acne
cleared and their eyes
adjusted to contact lenses
Then they swarmed

This is the year of their swarming

the air is black
the windows of our small town
are blurred we can barely see
for the black cloud eating its way
through our children

one by motorcycle
one by drowning
one by overdose
one by trainwheels
one by stabbing
one with her long hair shining
alone in a barn, yesterday

Kinereth Gensler

Plague is upon us, contagion
death of the first-born
and of the second-born
we are helpless to say goodbye, Sally
Michael, Danny, Karen, Kirk, Ann

We are helpless to help each other

THE AIR IN THIS ROOM

The children lift from their desks.
They glide to the chalkboard, buzzing.
Paintings are hung there: dreamings. Chalk dust
shimmers in sunlight.

The children hover. Their hands
dip over pencils. They dart like fish,
like dragonflies, the strange bright birds
they make poems from.

The air in this room is older than oceans.
Turned to the sun, the first plants breathed it.
Light seeped inward. The color of dreams
entered their leaves.

FROM THE RESIDUE OF MYTHOLOGIES

There is always a goat-herd,
a wet nurse, a simple woodman,
someone nameless
who saves the baby.

Always someone, ignorant
or defiant of orders,
who unbinds the child's ankles
or lifts him from the bulrushes.

Someone thwarts the king.
Someone is human.

Even now, on a pocked road
under exploding fires
a child is being snatched
from the sky's betrayal.

And later, in another
part of the forest,
someone will be left
who saves the baby,

if only a lonely she-wolf,
suckling the last, small man-things.

THE NEW YEAR
& Other Poems

Elizabeth Knies

as if life were only an instant, of course,
the dissolution of ourselves into others,
like a wedding party approaching the window.

-Pasternak

Elizabeth Knies

MEDITATION

Here, once more, and as if for the first time
the long boat-shaped leaves gone from the trees
sail off on a sea drained of color, a pure white sea.
How it was the same one year ago and a hundred years ago
on solitary mornings, remember.
It is almost too bright to bear watching —
the horizon is tilted up like a glittering bowl
ready to pour; and the watcher, transfixed, closes his eyes
to perceive as a blind man does for an instant
the shapes of things by feel and smell.
No, by a sense dropped inward on the eyelids,
a sixth sense, buried and exhumed by the sun,
the scene imprints itself on a plane removed.
Also like voices once heard and thought to be forgotten
forever, and now in these verses, coming to.

SOME SIGNS

The kingfisher on the wire is intellectual
and blue as a chord;
he takes in that scene, light and arrested
while the moon fills with words

and the cattails, feathered, move off
slowly into the night;
the brown rabbit's tail is a powderpuff
just as in stories! Could that be right?

On stilts the heron wades and fishes,
at midnight the doe freezes before the car;
Queen Anne's lace and jewelweed in the saltmarshes
rise like stars.

Gallant, you are walking on waterfalls
in the exhaled air where you have gone to forget.
Now that the fields are mown, the little foxes
peer curiously out, small as pets.

THE NEW YEAR

I cannot find my way
and the morning is beautiful,
after Christmas, after the drenching rain
that left the earth as damp as spring.

The red pine needles press into the mud
that ought to be covered with snow,
the sun slides down the birches
and bursts into flame at the tips of the branches.

Over it all the sky, washed out, a rag,
stretched to dry after the housecleaning;
nothing to do but sit and wait
for the arrival of the New Year.

It will come, as suddenly as before
and as slowly . . .as if it knew nothing of time;
as if time had nothing to do
with lips, hands, bodies and eyes

but suspended itself like a drop of water
containing the whole of the sky,
unwilling to be parted, even for an instant,
unable to conceive of the crossing-over.

COULD IT BE

Could it be that you will never change, even here,
that you will always look at the world with a nether lip
stuck out with displeasure and eyes darkened with fear
and a voice, strangled, clenched far inside like fingers?
The leaves have fallen under the snow;
even for you there are moments of repose
you who are so wily in your escape
sailing over polished floors sticking your head in rooms . . .
they will find you hanging upside down with the bats in the attic
if they bother to look. Unless you cast all this off
like ballast and become light and balloon-like rising in the air
where it doesn't matter what you are or why
and you look down laughing on your mutability.

Elizabeth Knies

HIGH SEA

I write you letters and my words don't say what I want them to
say
but here I take you and love you openly
it is easy
you rest lightly on my heart   rising and falling in the waves
you are a prisoner there   a prisoner without chains
riding out in the arms of a great sea-tide

this is what has been and will always be
you with me beneath the sky   marvelous and wide
beneath a moon that is whole and steadily rising
far out on the open sea   over the breathing earth

OSCURA

-for B.A. King

I study your profile against the light
holding carefully to the illuminated sky
the small box whose eye next to your eye
exacts from the world precise images.

You are deep in sun
as morning parts the field like a head of hair
and lays back through a channeled walkway
to the left and right the tasseled grasses.

The marsh-hen with her brood is there
hidden in mud-scent, not yet exposed,
while you wait breathless in a kind of oblivion
and the sky doubles down over you and them.

SONATINA

You do not hear me conversing with my cats
I do not see you rolling by on skates
pursued by (and perhaps pursuing) gentlemen in hats
while I whistle until my teeth fall on the plate.
If today brings 'just a memory of you'
it will be like all the others
                                        I do
wish you were sitting here with me instead of with another
on the Via Veneto or the Appian Way.
Then you would coin for me the remarkable phrase
"Cara mia!" It would be too true!
I watch instead the snowy trees filtered through blue
dusk; their tall stems, solemn and stately,
push into my heart like a vase

THERE

in a land bounded by blue rivers,
bounded and crossed-through and inclining seaward,
a land not unlike my own but untroubled by progress,
the emerald rocky meadows fit only for sheep
or cows or apple orchards, where each natural thing
follows its natural propensity. Men could live there,
but they would have to stop shaping *destiny*.
They would live according to the shape of the land.

GUARDIAN

Cannot you hear the chirping crickets sending
messages across the lawn? What is this, if not
summer's end, and weren't we lucky, truly lucky
to have seen it before it ended.

Something of you
I have here inside me where it will not break.
Incandescent images floating and yet steady
as market stalls piled with fruit. The pumpkins are ready,
they are set out on lawns like keepsakes.

THE BEAST

When I got out it was awful,
they thought they would have to kill me;
but they led me back and gently
burned lock and key.
I curled up in that flame,
it held me like a hand.
I would never be the same.

GREEN

It is not the right color green
it is a green of seizures
there are no apples in it
it is a green of dimes
and it holds nothing, like all false coins

POSSESSIONS

I have
a plain desk in a room
where sunlight penetrates
the long afternoon.
Afternoons of waiting.
The sea through the trees
is wet and separate.
It will not dry.
It is not a painting.
This is the real:
the quality of light, the passage
of birds, the patience of vows.

Elizabeth Knies

ABSENCE

You have withdrawn,
receded into memory once again.
What was your presence I put away
like a carefully folded letter.

You stepped out of me
as out of a room, but the door is ajar;
through it I see the days ahead open
like a path to a sepulchre.

NO MORE

There will be no more surprises
the pain increases
like water in a well
serene, unshatterable
until day draws another bucket up.

Stones stand stock still.
They make fences, rings and pathways.
They cannot be expected to console.

FALLEN AMONG THIEVES

It was at great expense, great personal expense
that I knew you.
I did not mark the cost
and now I am surprised to be bereft so,
left with nothing.
Like one who went among thieves
but did not know they were taking anything from him,
that is how I was with you.
You did not even deceive me.

IN WINTER

The earth is lightly held in winter,
the trees are its fingers   the light
falls gently through them, almost not held.
Even the stones could rise
but instead they lie there
on their bed of dry leaves.
Necessity lends them repose.

Elizabeth Knies

INTERSTICES

Cold room   winter
circles of light
the cast shadow
of rosemary dances on paper
the wind is bright
thin needles like pine
remote room   window sill
plants in sun

TO A FRIEND, NOW FAR AWAY

The mountains' blue smoke tells me you are gone
and my eyes mist over like the morning air.
You came to my door
and placed your heart on the threshold of the age.
The years ahead move outward like these mountains.
Will we meet again?
Will it be in this century?

Elizabeth Knies

HYDRANGEAS IN EARLY FALL

The bowl of hydrangeas is turbulent as clouds
set on a table; stuck among the clusters

wild phlox and asters, mauve and purple without depth
try to speak. Their efforts are pale and calming.

I put my lips near theirs and hear
a tinted verb in the shape of a petal

while my eyes close upon enormous vistas of pink
and open onto the sea, like balconies.

THE ANIMALS

come to us
from Paradise
look in their eyes
and you will see it
a starry memory
a perfect time
somewhere
in the great blue
a door opens
and they are sent down
to earth
claws
hoofs
feathers
wings
fur
they come
unceremoniously
a little awkwardly
without a word

YOU ARE MY EYES

You are my eyes
let me look through you

to that small scene
embellished in detail

a Persian miniature
where reds and blues

are royal, kingly
and lavished with gold leaf

Let you transform
my vision utterly

until the whole world
wears a grace

of light and air
of anonymity

of simple light and air

The Charm —

THE CHARM

Now you have gone *a husband, child, someone special*
friends are coming to the house again, *b memorial service*
friends I neglected for so long. *a*

Don't want them to feel sorry for you. You are trying to keep busy, to keep your mind off —

I am praying
that they will not notice
my pale preoccupation,

she invites them in to her home. There are so many

the slight movement of my lips
as I pass from table to door.
They fill the room

when the hum of their voices are heard it brings memories of the way things are. comforting.

with the light of their voices,
it is good
to sit as before

filling the glasses to the brim & drinking the whole lot — reminds her of happy times & holidays when there was much to fill them about & many toasts to make. this comforts her for a while.

and fill the glasses to overflowing
and drain them to the last drop.
For a time I am warm.

Like thick velvet, like a curtain,
simple words
hold back the dark.

The simple hellos and how are yous from familiar voices are just a black ya buffer to ease the pain of remembrance and of this loved one's death.

86

ARCHITECTURE

The space in the square
is not squared
space cannot be shaped
I thought, nor squared,
nor spaced, nor thought

The sun pours
into the space
but does not fill
and yet is full
it moves with the speed of light

no breath   no wind
we do not feel it pass by

How reckless all this is
all this invisible motion
the earth spinning through sky
the sky infinite   curving
in an endless curve
the planets and the stars
together in perfect time

this space   this shape   this thought

WITHIN THE YEAR

I make my circular way
along the cliffs
pushing aside
the stiff
knee-high, waist-high
spare
winter bushes.
Here
the blue-eyed grass
and black-eyed susan
once held sway,
here profuse
seaside roses
the rugged *rosa rugosa*
bloomed
and the bayberry
ripened its waxy fruit.
In these stubborn ledges
in spring
the most delicate
wild red columbines grew.
Now everything
is hushed but not bitter,
the tall grass is straw
the poison ivy inflicts
no terror.
Things are what they are,
the lifting
rocky sea
the moving sky
the staunch dry hedges
do not wither;
the red rose hips
what few remain
burn
at their center.